best of the best
ITALIAN

Publications International, Ltd.
Favorite Brand Name Recipes at www.fbnr.com

Pictured on the front cover: Spicy Italian Sausage & Penne Pasta *(page 66).*

Pictured on the back cover: Goat Cheese-Stuffed Figs *(page 26).*

ISBN-13: 978-1-4127-7798-8
ISBN-10: 1-4127-7798-4

Library of Congress Control Number: 2008940993

Manufactured in China.

8 7 6 5 4 3 2 1

Preparation/Cooking Times: Preparation times are based on the approximate amount
of time required to assemble the recipe before cooking, baking, chilling or serving.
These times include preparation steps such as measuring, chopping and mixing. The fact
that some preparations and cooking can be done simultaneously is taken into account.
Preparation of optional ingredients and serving suggestions is not included.

contents

incredible
appetizers & soups

Pan-Fried Polenta with Tomatoes and White Beans

2½ **cups chopped plum tomatoes**

  1 **cup canned white beans, rinsed and drained**

  ¼ **cup chopped fresh basil**

  ½ **teaspoon salt**

  ½ **teaspoon black pepper**

  2 **tablespoons olive oil**

  1 **package (16 ounces) prepared polenta, cut into ¼-inch-thick slices**

  ¼ **cup grated Parmesan cheese**

    Fresh basil leaves (optional)

1. Combine tomatoes, beans, basil, salt and pepper in medium bowl. Let stand at room temperature 15 minutes to blend flavors.

2. Heat 1 tablespoon oil in medium nonstick skillet over medium-high heat. Add half of polenta slices to skillet; cook about 4 minutes or until golden brown on both sides, turning once. Remove polenta from skillet. Repeat with remaining oil and polenta slices.

3. Arrange polenta on serving platter. Top with tomato-bean mixture. Sprinkle with Parmesan; garnish with basil leaves.

Makes 4 servings

Italian-Style Meatball Soup

½ **pound ground beef**
¼ **pound ground Italian sausage**
1 **large onion, finely chopped, divided**
⅓ **cup dry bread crumbs**
1 **egg**
½ **teaspoon salt**
4 **cups canned beef or vegetable broth**
2 **cups water**
1 **can (8 ounces) stewed tomatoes**
1 **can (8 ounces) pizza sauce**
2 **cups sliced cabbage**
1 **can (about 15 ounces) kidney beans, drained**
2 **medium carrots, sliced**
½ **cup frozen Italian green beans**

1. Combine beef, sausage, 2 tablespoons onion, bread crumbs, egg and salt in large bowl until well blended. Shape into 32 (1-inch) meatballs.

2. Brown half of meatballs in large skillet over medium heat, turning frequently. Remove from skillet; drain on paper towels. Repeat with remaining meatballs.

3. Bring broth, water, tomatoes and pizza sauce to a boil in Dutch oven over high heat. Add meatballs, remaining onion, cabbage, beans and carrots; bring to a boil. Reduce heat and simmer, uncovered, 20 minutes. Add green beans; return to a boil over high heat. Reduce heat and simmer, uncovered, 10 minutes.

Makes 8 servings

Italian-Style Meatball Soup

Grilled Summer Bruschetta

¾ cup WISH-BONE® 5 Cheese Italian Dressing
2 medium red, orange and/or yellow bell peppers, quartered
2 medium yellow squash and/or green zucchini, quartered lengthwise
1 tablespoon chopped fresh basil leaves
1 loaf Italian or French bread (about 15 inches long), cut ½-inch slices

1. In large shallow nonaluminum baking dish or plastic bag, pour ¼ cup Wish-Bone 5 Cheese Italian Dressing over red peppers and squash; turn to coat. Cover, or close bag, and marinate in refrigerator 15 minutes.

2. Meanwhile, brush bread with ¼ cup Dressing and grill or broil until golden. Remove vegetables from marinade, reserving marinade. Grill or broil vegetables, turning once and brushing with reserved marinade, 15 minutes or until vegetables are tender. Cool vegetables slightly, then coarsely chop.

3. In medium bowl, combine remaining ¼ cup Dressing, basil and, if desired, salt and ground black pepper to taste. Stir in vegetables and toss to coat. To serve, spoon vegetable mixture on toasted bread.   *Makes 30 appetizers*

Prep Time: 15 minutes
Marinate Time: 15 minutes
Cook Time: 20 minutes

Grilled Summer Bruschetta

Ravioli Minestrone

1 package (7 ounces) refrigerated three-cheese ravioli *or* 1 package (9 ounces) four-cheese ravioli

2 tablespoons olive oil

2 carrots, peeled and chopped

1 stalk celery, chopped

1 medium onion, chopped

2 cloves garlic, minced

6 cups water

1 can (about 15 ounces) chickpeas, rinsed and drained

1 can (about 14 ounces) diced tomatoes

3 tablespoons tomato paste

1 teaspoon dried basil

1 teaspoon dried oregano

¾ teaspoon salt

¾ teaspoon black pepper

1 medium zucchini, cut in half lengthwise, then cut into ¼-inch slices (about 2 cups)

1 package (10 ounces) baby spinach

1. Cook ravioli according to package directions; drain.

2. Meanwhile, heat oil in Dutch oven over medium-high heat. Add carrots, celery, onion and garlic; cook, stirring occasionally, about 5 minutes or until vegetables are softened.

3. Stir in water, chickpeas, tomatoes, tomato paste, basil, oregano, salt and pepper. Bring to a boil; reduce heat and simmer 15 minutes or until vegetables are tender. Add zucchini; cook 5 minutes. Stir in spinach; cook 2 minutes or just until spinach wilts. Stir in ravioli.

Makes 8 servings

Prep Time: 20 minutes
Cook Time: 27 minutes

Ravioli Minestrone

Asparagus & Prosciutto Antipasto

12 asparagus spears (about 8 ounces)
2 ounces cream cheese, softened
¼ cup (1 ounce) crumbled blue cheese or goat cheese
¼ teaspoon black pepper
1 package (3 to 4 ounces) thinly sliced prosciutto

1. Trim and discard tough ends of asparagus spears. Simmer asparagus in salted water in large skillet 4 to 5 minutes or until crisp-tender. Drain; immediately immerse in cold water to stop cooking. Drain; pat dry with paper towels.

2. Meanwhile, combine cheeses and pepper in small bowl; mix well. Cut prosciutto slices in half crosswise. Spread cream cheese mixture evenly over one side of each prosciutto slice.

3. Wrap each asparagus spear with one prosciutto slice. Serve at room temperature or slightly chilled. *Makes 12 appetizers*

Caponata

1 pound eggplant, cut into ½-inch cubes
3 large cloves garlic, minced
¼ cup olive oil
1 can (14½ ounces) DEL MONTE® Diced Tomatoes with Basil, Garlic & Oregano
1 medium green pepper, finely chopped
1 can (2¼ ounces) chopped ripe olives, drained
2 tablespoons lemon juice
1 teaspoon dried basil, crushed
1 baguette French bread, cut into ¼-inch slices

1. Cook eggplant and garlic in oil in large skillet over medium heat 5 minutes. Season with salt and pepper, if desired.

2. Stir in remaining ingredients except bread. Cook, uncovered, 10 minutes or until thickened.

3. Cover and chill. Serve with bread.

Makes approximately 4½ cups

Asparagus & Prosciutto Antipasto

Italian Wedding Soup

    1 tablespoon olive oil
    1 pound bulk Italian sausage*
  ½ cup chopped onion
  ½ cup chopped carrot
    1 teaspoon Italian seasoning
 7½ cups reduced-sodium chicken broth
    3 cups packed chopped kale
    1 cup uncooked ditalini or other small shaped pasta
      Grated Parmesan cheese

If bulk sausage is not available, use sausage links and remove the casings.

1. Heat oil in Dutch oven or large saucepan over medium-high heat. Add sausage, onion, carrot and Italian seasoning; cook and stir about 4 minutes or until sausage is no longer pink. Drain fat.

2. Stir in broth and kale; bring to a boil over high heat. Stir in ditalini. Reduce heat to medium-low; simmer, partially covered, about 9 minutes or until pasta is tender. Sprinkle with Parmesan.

Makes 6 servings

Kale is a member of the cabbage family. It comes in many varieties and colors (most commonly deep green) and has a mild cabbage flavor. Store kale in a perforated plastic bag in the refrigerator for two to three days. Wash kale well and remove the tough center stalks before cooking.

Italian Wedding Soup

Fried Calamari with Tartar Sauce

Tartar Sauce (recipe follows)
1 pound cleaned squid (body tubes, tentacles or combination)
¾ cup dry plain bread crumbs
1 egg
1 tablespoon milk
Vegetable oil
Lemon wedges (optional)

1. Prepare Tartar Sauce; set aside. Rinse squid under cold running water. Cut each body tube crosswise into ¼-inch rings. Pat pieces dry with paper towels.

2. Spread bread crumbs on plate. Beat egg and milk in small bowl. Add squid pieces; stir to coat well. Dip squid in bread crumbs; place in shallow bowl or on waxed paper. Let stand 10 to 15 minutes before frying.

3. To deep fry squid, heat 1½ inches oil in large saucepan to 350°F. (Caution: Squid will pop and spatter during frying; do not stand too close to pan.) Fry 8 to 10 pieces of squid at a time 45 seconds or until golden brown.* Adjust heat to maintain temperature of oil. Remove squid with slotted spoon; drain on paper towels. Repeat with remaining squid. *Do not overcook squid or it will become tough.*

4. Serve hot with Tartar Sauce and lemon, if desired.

Makes 2 to 3 servings

*To shallow fry squid, heat about ¼ inch oil in large skillet over medium-high heat; reduce heat to medium. Add single layer of squid to oil without crowding. Cook 1 minute per side or until golden brown. Drain on paper towels.

Tartar Sauce

1⅓ cups mayonnaise
2 tablespoons chopped fresh parsley
1 green onion, thinly sliced
1 tablespoon drained capers, minced
1 small sweet gherkin or pickle, minced

Combine all ingredients in small bowl; mix well. Cover; refrigerate until ready to serve.

Makes about 1⅓ cups

Fried Calamari with Tartar Sauce

Easy Tomato Minestrone

3 slices bacon, diced
½ cup chopped onion
1 clove garlic, minced
3½ cups water
2 cans (10½ ounces each) condensed beef broth, undiluted
1 can (15 ounces) Great Northern beans, undrained
1 can (6 ounces) CONTADINA® Tomato Paste
½ cup dry pasta shells, macaroni or vermicelli, broken into 1-inch pieces
¼ cup chopped fresh parsley
1 teaspoon dried oregano leaves, crushed
1 teaspoon dried basil leaves, crushed
¼ teaspoon black pepper
1 package (16 ounces) frozen mixed Italian vegetables
½ cup grated Parmesan cheese (optional)

1. Sauté bacon, onion and garlic in large saucepan until onion is translucent.

2. Stir in water, broth, beans and liquid, tomato paste, pasta, parsley, oregano, basil and pepper; heat to boiling.

3. Reduce heat; simmer 15 minutes. Mix in vegetables; cook additional 10 minutes. Serve with Parmesan cheese, if desired.

Makes about 8 servings

Easy Tomato Minestrone

Hearty Tortellini Soup

1 small red onion, chopped
2 medium carrots, chopped
2 ribs celery, thinly sliced
1 small zucchini, chopped
2 plum tomatoes, chopped
2 cloves garlic, minced
2 cans (14½ ounces each) chicken broth
1 can (15 to 19 ounces) red kidney beans, rinsed and drained
2 tablespoons *French's®* Worcestershire Sauce
1 package (9 ounces) refrigerated tortellini pasta

1. Heat *2 tablespoons oil* in 6-quart saucepot or Dutch oven over medium-high heat. Add vegetables, tomatoes and garlic. Cook and stir 5 minutes or until vegetables are crisp-tender.

2. Add broth, *½ cup water,* beans and Worcestershire. Heat to boiling. Stir in pasta. Return to boiling. Cook 5 minutes or until pasta is tender, stirring occasionally. Serve with crusty bread and grated Parmesan cheese, if desired.   *Makes 4 servings*

Prep Time: 15 minutes
Cook Time: 10 minutes

Tuscan White Bean Crostini

2 cans (about 15 ounces each) cannellini or Great Northern beans, rinsed and drained
½ large red bell pepper, finely chopped *or* ⅓ cup finely chopped roasted red bell pepper
⅓ cup finely chopped onion
⅓ cup red wine vinegar
3 tablespoons chopped fresh parsley
1 tablespoon olive oil
2 cloves garlic, minced
½ teaspoon dried oregano
¼ teaspoon black pepper
18 slices French bread, about ¼ inch thick

1. Combine beans, bell pepper and onion in large bowl.

2. Whisk vinegar, parsley, oil, garlic, oregano and black pepper in small bowl. Pour over bean mixture; toss to coat. Cover; refrigerate 2 hours or overnight.

3. Preheat broiler. Arrange bread slices in single layer on large ungreased baking sheet or broiler pan. Broil, 6 to 8 inches from heat, 30 to 45 seconds or until bread slices are lightly toasted. Cool completely.

4. Top each toasted bread slice with about 3 tablespoons bean mixture.   *Makes 18 crostini*

Marinated Antipasto

¼ **cup extra-virgin olive oil**
2 **tablespoons balsamic vinegar**
1 **clove garlic, minced**
½ **teaspoon sugar**
½ **teaspoon salt**
¼ **teaspoon black pepper**
1 **pint (2 cups) cherry tomatoes**
1 **can (14 ounces) quartered artichoke hearts, drained**
8 **ounces small balls or cubes fresh mozzarella cheese**
1 **cup drained pitted kalamata olives**
¼ **cup sliced fresh basil**
Lettuce leaves

1. Whisk oil, vinegar, garlic, sugar, salt and pepper in medium bowl until well blended. Add tomatoes, artichokes, mozzarella, olives and basil; toss to coat. Let stand at least 30 minutes.

2. Line platter with lettuce. Arrange antipasto over lettuce; serve at room temperature.   *Makes about 5 cups*

Serving Suggestion: Serve antipasto with toothpicks or spoon over Bibb lettuce leaves for a first-course salad.

Caramelized Onion Focaccia

2 tablespoons plus 1 teaspoon olive oil, divided
4 medium onions, cut in half and thinly sliced
½ teaspoon salt
2 tablespoons water
1 tablespoon chopped fresh rosemary leaves
¼ teaspoon black pepper
1 loaf (16 ounces) frozen bread dough, thawed
1 cup (4 ounces) shredded fontina cheese
¼ cup grated Parmesan cheese

1. Heat 2 tablespoons oil in large skillet over medium-high heat. Add onions and salt; cook about 10 minutes or until onions begin to brown, stirring occasionally. Stir in water. Reduce heat to medium; partially cover and cook about 20 minutes or until onions are deep golden brown, stirring occasionally. Remove from heat; stir in rosemary and pepper. Let cool slightly.

2. Meanwhile, brush 13×9-inch baking pan with remaining 1 teaspoon oil. Roll out dough to 13×9-inch rectangle on lightly floured surface. Transfer dough to prepared pan; cover and let rise in warm, draft-free place 30 minutes.

3. Preheat oven to 375°F. Prick dough all over with fork. Sprinkle fontina over dough; top with caramelized onions. Sprinkle with Parmesan.

4. Bake 18 to 20 minutes or until golden brown. Remove from pan to wire rack. Cut into pieces; serve warm.   *Makes 12 servings*

Caramelized Onion Focaccia

Chicken Tortellini Soup

6 cups chicken broth

1 package (9 ounces) refrigerated cheese and spinach or three-cheese tortellini

1 package (about 6 ounces) refrigerated fully cooked chicken breast strips, cut into bite-size pieces

2 cups baby spinach

4 to 6 tablespoons grated Parmesan cheese

1 tablespoon chopped fresh chives *or* 2 tablespoons sliced green onion

1. Bring broth to a boil in large saucepan over high heat; add tortellini. Reduce heat to medium; cook 5 minutes. Stir in chicken and spinach.

2. Reduce heat to low; cook 3 minutes or until chicken is heated through. Sprinkle with Parmesan and chives.   *Makes 4 servings*

Tomato and Caper Crostini

1 French roll, cut into 8 slices

2 plum tomatoes, finely chopped

1 tablespoon extra-virgin olive oil

1 tablespoon plus 1½ teaspoons capers, drained

1½ teaspoons dried basil

¼ cup (1 ounce) crumbled feta cheese with sun-dried tomatoes and basil

1. Preheat oven to 350°F.

2. Place bread slices on ungreased baking sheet in single layer. Bake 15 minutes or just until golden brown. Cool completely.

3. Meanwhile, combine tomatoes, oil, capers and basil in small bowl; mix well. Just before serving, spoon about 1 tablespoon tomato mixture on each bread slice; sprinkle with feta.

Makes 4 servings

Chicken Tortellini Soup

Goat Cheese-Stuffed Figs

7 fresh firm ripe figs
7 slices prosciutto
1 package (4 ounces) goat cheese
  Ground black pepper

1. Preheat broiler. Line baking sheet or broiler pan with foil. Cut figs in half lengthwise. Cut prosciutto slices in half lengthwise to create 14 pieces (about 4 inches long and 1 inch wide).

2. Scoop 1 teaspoon goat cheese onto cut side of each fig half. Wrap prosciutto slice around fig half. Sprinkle with pepper.

3. Broil about 4 minutes or until cheese softens and figs are heated through. *Makes 4 to 6 servings*

Bruschetta

1 can (14½ ounces) DEL MONTE® PETITE CUT™ Diced Tomatoes, drained
2 tablespoons chopped fresh basil *or* ½ teaspoon dried basil
1 small clove garlic, finely minced
½ French bread baguette, cut into ⅜-inch-thick slices
2 tablespoons olive oil

1. Combine tomatoes, basil and garlic in 1-quart bowl; cover and refrigerate at least ½ hour.

2. Preheat broiler. Place bread slices on baking sheet; lightly brush both sides of bread with oil. Broil until lightly toasted, turning to toast both sides. Cool on wire rack.

3. Bring tomato mixture to room temperature. Spoon tomato mixture over bread and serve immediately. Sprinkle with additional fresh basil leaves, if desired. *Makes 8 appetizer servings*

Note: For a fat-free version, omit the olive oil. For a lower-fat variation, spray the bread with olive oil cooking spray.

Goat Cheese-Stuffed Figs

Eggplant Rolls

1 large eggplant (about 1¼ pounds)
3 tablespoons extra-virgin olive oil
   Salt and black pepper
1 cup whole milk ricotta cheese
½ cup grated Asiago cheese
¼ cup julienned or chopped sun-dried tomatoes packed in oil
¼ cup chopped fresh basil or Italian parsley
⅛ teaspoon red pepper flakes
   Cherry tomatoes, halved (optional)
   Fresh thyme or basil sprigs (optional)

1. Preheat broiler. Trim off stem end from eggplant; peel eggplant, if desired. Cut eggplant lengthwise into 6 slices (about ¼ inch thick). Brush both sides of eggplant slices with oil; sprinkle with salt and pepper to taste. Place on rack of broiler pan.

2. Broil eggplant 4 inches from heat source 4 to 5 minutes per side or until golden brown and slightly softened. Let cool to room temperature.

3. Combine ricotta, Asiago, sun-dried tomatoes, basil and red pepper flakes in small bowl; mix well.

4. Spread cheese mixture evenly over cooled eggplant slices. Roll up and cut each roll in half diagonally. Arrange seam side down on serving platter; garnish with tomatoes and thyme. Serve warm or at room temperature. *Makes 6 appetizer servings*

Eggplant Rolls

Margherita Panini Bites

1 loaf (16 ounces) ciabatta or crusty Italian bread, cut into 16 (½-inch) slices

8 teaspoons pesto

16 fresh basil leaves

8 slices mozzarella cheese

24 thin slices plum tomato (about 3 tomatoes)

Olive oil

1. Preheat indoor grill. Spread one side of 8 slices bread with 1 teaspoon pesto. Top with 2 basil leaves, 1 mozzarella slice and 3 tomato slices. Top with remaining bread slices.

2. Brush both sides of sandwiches lightly with oil. Grill sandwiches 5 minutes or until lightly browned and cheese is melted.

3. Cut each sandwich into 4 pieces. Serve warm.

Makes 32 panini bites

BelGioioso® Fresh Mozzarella Ciliegine and Grape Tomato Appetizer

12 ounces BELGIOIOSO® Fresh Mozzarella Ciliegine

1 pint grape tomatoes

¾ cup Italian vinaigrette

16 small wooden skewers

Freshly ground black pepper and salt

Drain liquid from BELGIOIOSO® Fresh Mozzarella Ciliegine, reserving some for storing any leftover cheese. Place ciliegine in large bowl. Rinse grape tomatoes well and remove any stems. Drain well and add to bowl with cheese. Add vinaigrette to bowl and toss gently with cheese and tomatoes.

Alternate grape tomatoes and ciliegine on skewers. Top with black pepper and salt then serve.

Makes 8 servings

Margherita Panini Bites

sensational
salads & vegetables

Olive and Broccoli Salad with Italian Tomato Dressing

10 ounces dry rotini or bow tie pasta
1 can (6 ounces) CONTADINA® Tomato Paste
1 cup Italian dressing
½ teaspoon hot pepper sauce
3 cups broccoli flowerets, cooked
1 cup halved pitted ripe olives, drained
1 medium red onion, cut into thin strips
½ cup diced cucumber
2 tablespoons pine nuts, toasted

1. Cook pasta according to package directions; drain and chill.

2. Meanwhile, combine tomato paste, dressing and hot pepper sauce in small bowl.

3. Combine pasta, broccoli, olives, onion and cucumber in large bowl; toss well. Add tomato paste mixture; mix lightly. Transfer salad to platter; sprinkle with pine nuts.   *Makes 8 servings*

Prep Time: 10 minutes
Cook Time: 12 minutes

Italian Vegetarian Grill

2 large bell peppers, cut into quarters
2 medium zucchini, cut crosswise into ½-inch thick slices
8 ounces asparagus (about 10 spears)
1 large red onion, cut into ½-inch-thick rounds
¼ cup olive oil
1½ teaspoons salt, divided
1 teaspoon Italian seasoning
½ teaspoon black pepper, divided
4 cups water
1 cup uncooked polenta
4 ounces goat cheese

1. Arrange bell peppers, zucchini and asparagus in single layer on baking sheet. To hold onion together securely, pierce slices horizontally with metal skewers. Add to baking sheet. Combine oil, ½ teaspoon salt, Italian seasoning and ¼ teaspoon black pepper in small bowl. Brush mixture generously over vegetables, turning to coat all sides.

2. Prepare grill for direct cooking. Meanwhile, bring water and remaining 1 teaspoon salt to a boil in large saucepan over high heat. Gradually whisk in polenta. Reduce heat to medium; cook and stir until polenta thickens and begins to pull away from side of pan. Stir in remaining ¼ teaspoon black pepper. Cover and keep warm.

3. Grill vegetables over medium-high heat, covered, 10 to 15 minutes or until tender, turning once. Place bell peppers in large bowl; cover and let stand 5 minutes to loosen skin. When cool enough to handle, peel off charred skin. Cut all vegetables into bite-size pieces.

4. Pour polenta into serving bowls; top with vegetables and sprinkle with goat cheese. *Makes 4 servings*

Italian Vegetarian Grill

Roasted Peppers and Potatoes

 2 pounds small red potatoes, quartered
 1 large red bell pepper, cut into 1½-inch chunks
 1 large yellow or orange bell pepper, cut into 1½-inch chunks
 1 large red onion, cut into 1-inch pieces
 ¼ cup olive oil
 3 cloves garlic, minced
 ¾ teaspoon salt
 ¼ teaspoon black pepper
 ¼ teaspoon dried basil
 ¼ teaspoon dried oregano

1. Preheat oven to 375°F.

2. Place potatoes, bell peppers and onion in large resealable food storage bag. Combine oil, garlic, salt, pepper, basil and oregano in small bowl; pour over vegetables. Seal bag; shake until vegetables are evenly coated. Spread on baking sheet.

3. Bake 50 minutes or until potatoes are tender and beginning to brown, stirring every 15 minutes.   *Makes 4 to 6 servings*

Green Bean Salad

 1 pound fresh green beans, trimmed
 3 tablespoons lemon juice
 1 tablespoon FILIPPO BERIO® Extra Virgin Olive Oil
 ½ teaspoon dried oregano leaves
   Salt

In medium saucepan, cook beans in boiling salted water 10 to 15 minutes or until tender. Drain well; cool slightly. In small bowl, whisk together lemon juice, olive oil and oregano. Pour over green beans; toss until lightly coated. Cover; refrigerate several hours or overnight before serving. Season to taste with salt.

Makes 6 servings

Note: Salad may also be served as an appetizer.

Roasted Peppers and Potatoes

Sweet Italian Marinated Vegetable Salad

½ can (14 ounces) quartered artichoke hearts, drained
6 ounces grape or cherry tomatoes, halved
½ cup chopped green bell pepper
¼ cup finely chopped red onion
2 ounces mozzarella, cut into ¼-inch cubes
2 tablespoons white vinegar
1 tablespoon chopped fresh oregano *or* 1 teaspoon dried oregano
2 teaspoons sugar
⅛ teaspoon salt
⅛ teaspoon dried pepper flakes

Combine all ingredients in medium bowl. Serve immediately or chill 1 hour to blend flavors.   *Makes 4 servings*

Sautéed Swiss Chard

1 large bunch Swiss chard or kale (about 1 pound)
1 tablespoon olive oil
3 cloves garlic, minced
¾ teaspoon salt
¼ teaspoon black pepper
1 tablespoon balsamic vinegar (optional)
¼ cup pine nuts, toasted

1. Rinse chard in cold water; shake off excess water but do not dry. Finely chop stems and coarsely chop leaves.

2. Heat oil in large saucepan or Dutch oven over medium heat. Add garlic; cook and stir 2 minutes. Add chard, salt and pepper; cover and cook 2 minutes or until chard begins to wilt. Uncover; cook and stir about 5 minutes or until chard is evenly wilted.

3. Stir in vinegar, if desired. Sprinkle with pine nuts just before serving.
Makes 4 servings

Sweet Italian Marinated Vegetable Salad

Pesto Rice Salad

2 cups MINUTE® White Rice, uncooked
1 package (7 ounces) basil pesto sauce
1 cup cherry tomatoes, halved
8 ounces whole-milk mozzarella cheese, cut into ½-inch cubes
⅓ cup shredded Parmesan cheese
Toasted pine nuts (optional)

Prepare rice according to package directions. Place in large bowl. Let stand 10 minutes. Add pesto sauce; mix well. Gently stir in tomatoes and cheese. Serve warm, or cover and refrigerate until ready to serve. Sprinkle with pine nuts, if desired.

Makes 6 servings

Tip: For a heartier meal, add 1 package (6 ounces) grilled chicken breast strips to the prepared salad.

note

To toast pine nuts, spread them in a single layer in a heavy-bottomed skillet. Cook over medium heat 1 to 2 minutes, stirring frequently, until the nuts are lightly browned. Remove from the skillet immediately. Cool before using.

Pesto Rice Salad

Ravioli Panzanella

1 package (9 ounces) refrigerated fresh cheese ravioli or tortellini
2 tablespoons olive oil
2 teaspoons white wine vinegar
⅛ teaspoon black pepper
1 cup halved grape tomatoes *or* 1 large tomato, cored and chopped
½ cup sliced pimiento-stuffed green olives
¼ cup finely chopped celery
1 large shallot, finely chopped *or* ¼ cup finely chopped red onion
¼ cup finely chopped Italian parsley

1. Cook ravioli according to package directions; drain. Transfer to large serving bowl; set aside to cool 10 minutes.

2. Whisk oil, vinegar and pepper in small bowl until well blended. Add to ravioli with tomatoes, olives, celery and shallot; toss gently. Sprinkle with parsley. *Makes 6 servings*

Tuna and Bean Salad

1 can (about 15 ounces) cannellini beans, rinsed and drained
1 can (8 ounces) broad or lima beans, rinsed and drained
½ red onion, thinly sliced
2 cans (6½ ounces each) tuna in oil, undrained
⅓ cup olive oil
2 tablespoons red wine vinegar
   Black pepper
½ cup pitted black olives
2 tablespoons chopped fresh Italian parsley
   Italian bread (optional)

1. Combine beans and onion in large bowl. Add tuna; break into large flakes with fork.

2. Blend oil, vinegar and pepper to taste in small bowl; pour over tuna mixture. Add olives and parsley; mix well. Serve with bread, if desired. *Makes 6 servings*

Ravioli Panzanella

Calamari Salad

¼ cup plus 1 tablespoon extra-virgin olive oil, divided
1½ pounds cleaned fresh squid, bodies only
   Juice of 1 lemon
1 can (about 15 ounces) cannellini beans, rinsed and drained
1 cup thinly sliced celery
1 cup thinly sliced red bell pepper
½ cup thinly sliced white onion
3 tablespoons red wine vinegar
2 tablespoons chopped Italian parsley
1 tablespoon chopped fresh basil
1 tablespoon chopped fresh oregano
2 cloves garlic, minced
1 teaspoon salt
½ teaspoon red pepper flakes

1. Heat 1 tablespoon oil in large nonstick skillet over medium-high heat. Cook squid about 2 minutes per side. Let cool slightly; cut into rings. Place in large bowl; drizzle with lemon juice. Stir in beans, celery, bell pepper and onion.

2. Whisk vinegar, parsley, basil, oregano, garlic, salt and red pepper flakes in small bowl until blended. Slowly whisk in remaining ¼ cup oil until well blended. Pour dressing over squid mixture; toss gently to coat. Refrigerate at least 1 hour. Serve chilled or at room temperature. *Makes 6 servings*

Tuscan Bean, Chicken & Spinach Salad

1 can (19 ounces) cannellini or white kidney beans, rinsed and
   drained
½ cup WISH-BONE® Italian Dressing
4 boneless, skinless chicken breast halves (about 1¼ pounds)
1 bag (9 ounces) baby spinach leaves
2 large plum tomatoes, thinly sliced

1. In small bowl, combine beans and ¼ cup Wish-Bone Italian Dressing; set aside.

2. Grill or broil chicken, turning once and brushing with remaining ¼ cup Dressing until chicken is thoroughly cooked. Thinly slice chicken.

3. On serving platter, arrange spinach, then top with chicken, tomatoes and bean mixture. Serve, if desired, with additional Dressing and fresh ground black pepper.   *Makes 4 servings*

Prep Time: 15 minutes
Cook Time: 10 minutes

Scalloped Potatoes with Gorgonzola

1½ **cups whipping cream**
1 **can (14½ ounces) chicken broth**
4 **teaspoons minced garlic**
1½ **teaspoons dried sage leaves**
1 **cup BELGIOIOSO® Gorgonzola Cheese**
2¼ **pounds russet potatoes, peeled, halved, thinly sliced**

Preheat oven to 375°F. Simmer whipping cream, chicken broth, garlic and sage in heavy medium saucepan 5 minutes until slightly thickened. Add BELGIOIOSO® Gorgonzola and stir until melted. Remove from heat.

Place potatoes in large bowl and season with salt and pepper. Arrange half of potatoes in 13×9×2-inch glass baking dish. Pour half of cream mixture over potatoes. Repeat layering with remaining potatoes and cream mixture. Bake until potatoes are tender, about 1¼ hours. Let stand 15 minutes before serving.   *Makes 8 servings*

Grilled Tri-Colored Pepper Salad

1 *each* large red, yellow and green bell pepper, cut into quarters
⅓ cup extra-virgin olive oil
3 tablespoons balsamic vinegar
2 cloves garlic, minced
¼ teaspoon salt
¼ teaspoon black pepper
1½ ounces (about ⅓ cup) crumbled goat cheese
¼ cup thinly sliced fresh basil

1. Prepare grill for direct cooking.

2. Place bell peppers, skin side down, on grid over high heat. Grill, covered, 10 to 12 minutes or until skin is charred. Place charred bell peppers in paper bag. Close bag; set aside to cool 10 to 15 minutes. Remove and discard skin.

3. Place bell peppers in shallow glass serving dish. Combine oil, vinegar, garlic, salt and black pepper in small bowl; whisk until well combined. Pour over bell peppers. Let stand 30 minutes at room temperature. (Or cover and refrigerate up to 24 hours. Bring salad to room temperature before serving.)

4. Sprinkle salad with goat cheese and basil just before serving.

Makes 4 to 6 servings

Grilled Tri-Colored Pepper Salad

Broccoli Italian Style

1¼ pounds broccoli
2 tablespoons lemon juice
1 tablespoon extra-virgin olive oil
1 clove garlic, minced
1 teaspoon chopped fresh Italian parsley
Black pepper

1. Trim broccoli, discarding tough stems. Cut broccoli into florets. Peel broccoli stems; cut into ½-inch slices.

2. Bring 1 quart water to a boil in large saucepan over high heat. Add broccoli; return to a boil. Reduce heat to medium-high. Cook, uncovered, 3 to 5 minutes or until broccoli is fork-tender. Drain; transfer to serving dish.

3. Combine lemon juice, oil, garlic, parsley and pepper in small bowl. Pour over broccoli; toss to coat. Let stand, covered, 1 to 2 hours before serving.   *Makes 4 servings*

Tuscan Bread Salad (Panzanella Salad)

1½ pounds tomatoes, chopped (about 4 large)
1 cucumber, peeled and chopped
1 small red onion, thinly sliced
1 cup WISH-BONE® Italian Dressing
3 tablespoons drained capers
4 cups day-old, cubed Italian bread (about 6 ounces)

1. In large bowl, combine all ingredients except bread. Add bread and toss until evenly coated. Chill at least 1 hour before serving.
Makes 9 (1-cup) servings

Prep Time: 10 minutes
Chill Time: 1 hour

Broccoli Italian Style

Peperonata

  2 tablespoons extra-virgin olive oil
  4 large red, yellow or orange bell peppers, cut into thin strips
  2 cloves garlic, coarsely chopped
 12 pimiento-stuffed green olives or pitted black olives,
      cut into halves
  2 to 3 tablespoons white or red wine vinegar
  ¼ teaspoon salt
  ¼ teaspoon black pepper

1. Heat oil in large skillet over medium-high heat. Add bell peppers; cook 8 to 9 minutes or until edges begin to brown, stirring frequently.

2. Reduce heat to medium. Add garlic; cook and stir 1 to 2 minutes. *Do not allow garlic to brown.* Add olives, vinegar, salt and black pepper. Cook 1 to 2 minutes or until all liquid has evaporated.

Makes 4 to 5 servings

note

Peperonata is a very versatile dish. It can be served hot as a condiment with bread or crackers or as a side with meat dishes. It can also be chilled and served as part of an antipasti selection.

Peperonata

White Bean and Orzo Salad

¾ cup (6 ounces) uncooked orzo pasta
1 can (about 15 ounces) navy beans, rinsed and drained
1 cup packed spinach leaves, coarsely chopped
½ cup chopped roasted bell peppers
¼ cup Italian salad dressing
3 tablespoons capers, rinsed and drained
3 tablespoons chopped fresh basil
¼ cup crumbled feta cheese

1. Cook orzo according to package directions; drain.

2. Meanwhile, combine beans, spinach, peppers, dressing, capers and basil in large bowl.

3. Add orzo to bean mixture; sprinkle with feta.

Makes 6 servings

Tomato, Prosciutto & Fresh Mozzarella Salad

1 package (10 ounces) DOLE® Organic Salad Blend Spring Mix with Herbs or Baby Lettuces Salad
1 cup yellow and red pear or cherry tomatoes, halved
1½ ounces prosciutto, chopped *or* 5 strips bacon, cooked, drained and crumbled
4 ounces fresh mozzarella cheese, drained and cut into bits or regular mozzarella cheese, cut into julienne strips
1 cup sliced red onion
1 cup croutons
¼ cup prepared balsamic vinaigrette dressing

• Combine salad blend, tomatoes, prosciutto, cheese, onion and croutons in large bowl.

• Pour vinaigrette over salad; toss to evenly coat.

Makes 4 servings

Prep Time: 20 minutes

White Bean and Orzo Salad

Marinated Tomato Salad

2 cups cherry tomatoes, cut into halves
1 large cucumber, cut in half lengthwise and sliced
1 large yellow or red bell pepper, cut into strips
3 slices red onion, quartered
2 tablespoons balsamic vinegar
1 tablespoon olive oil
½ teaspoon dried basil
¼ to ½ teaspoon onion salt
¼ teaspoon garlic powder
¼ teaspoon dried oregano

1. Combine tomatoes, cucumber, bell pepper and onion in large bowl.

2. Whisk vinegar, oil, basil, onion salt, garlic powder and oregano in small bowl until well blended. Pour over vegetables; mix well.

Makes 4 to 6 servings

Mixed Spring Vegetable Salad

8 ounces fresh green beans, trimmed and cut into thirds
1 medium zucchini (about ½ pound), sliced
1 large tomato *or* 3 plum tomatoes, sliced
3 tablespoons FILIPPO BERIO® Extra Virgin Olive Oil
3 tablespoons lemon juice
Salt and freshly ground black pepper

Cook or steam green beans and zucchini separately until tender-crisp. Cover; refrigerate until chilled. Stir in tomato. Just before serving, drizzle olive oil and lemon juice over vegetables. Season to taste with salt and pepper.

Makes 6 servings

Marinated Tomato Salad

perfect pasta & rice

Classic Fettuccine Alfredo

12 ounces uncooked fettuccine
⅔ cup whipping cream
6 tablespoons unsalted butter
½ teaspoon salt
White pepper
Ground nutmeg
1 cup grated Parmesan cheese
2 tablespoons chopped fresh Italian parsley

1. Cook fettucine according to package directions; drain. Return to saucepan; cover and keep warm.

2. Meanwhile, heat cream and butter in large heavy skillet over medium-low heat until butter melts and mixture bubbles, stirring frequently. Cook and stir 2 minutes. Stir in salt, pepper and nutmeg. Remove from heat. Gradually stir in Parmesan until well blended and smooth. Return to heat briefly to completely blend cheese, if necessary. (Do not let sauce bubble or cheese will become lumpy and tough.)

3. Pour sauce over fettucine; cook and stir over low heat 2 to 3 minutes or until sauce is thickened and fettucine is evenly coated. Sprinkle with parsley. Serve immediately.

Makes 4 servings

Winter Squash Risotto

- **2 tablespoons olive oil**
- **2 cups cubed butternut or delicata squash (1 small butternut squash or 1 medium delicata)**
- **1 large shallot, chopped, or 1 very small onion, finely chopped**
- **½ teaspoon paprika**
- **¼ teaspoon salt**
- **¼ teaspoon dried thyme**
- **¼ teaspoon black pepper**
- **1 cup arborio rice**
- **¼ cup dry white wine (optional)**
- **4 to 5 cups hot chicken broth**
- **½ cup grated Parmesan or Romano cheese**

1. Heat oil in large skillet over medium heat. Add squash; cook and stir 3 minutes. Add shallot; cook 3 to 4 minutes or until squash gives when knife is inserted but is not completely tender. Stir in paprika, salt, thyme and pepper. Add rice; stir to coat with oil.

2. Add wine, if desired; cook and stir until wine evaporates. Reduce heat to low. Add ½ cup broth; cook over medium heat, stirring occasionally. When rice is almost dry, stir in another ½ cup broth. Stir in remaining broth, ½ cup at a time, until rice is creamy and tender. (Total cooking time will be 20 to 30 minutes.) Stir in Parmesan. Serve immediately.   *Makes 4 to 6 servings*

Winter Squash Risotto

Rigatoni with Sausage & Beans

    1 pound sweet Italian sausage links, cut in ½-inch pieces
    1 jar (1 pound 10 ounces) RAGÚ® Chunky Gardenstyle Pasta Sauce
    1 can (19 ounces) cannellini or white kidney beans, rinsed and
        drained
    ⅛ to ¼ teaspoon dried rosemary leaves, crushed (optional)
    1 box (16 ounces) rigatoni or ziti pasta, cooked and drained

1. In 12-inch skillet, brown sausage over medium-high heat; drain. Stir in Ragú Pasta Sauce, beans and rosemary.

2. Bring to a boil over high heat. Reduce heat to low and simmer uncovered, stirring occasionally, 10 minutes or until sausage is done. Serve over hot pasta.   *Makes 4 servings*

Prep Time: 5 minutes
Cook Time: 20 minutes

Tagliatelle with Creamy Sauce

    7 to 8 ounces tagliatelle pasta, cooked, drained
    1 cup GALBANI® Mascarpone cheese
    1 package (10 ounces) frozen peas, cooked, drained
    2 ounces (½ cup) finely chopped GALBANI® Prosciutto di Parma
 1½ cups (6 ounces) shredded mozzarella cheese
    Butter or margarine

Layer half of the tagliatelle in buttered 9×9-inch baking dish. Spoon half of the Mascarpone over tagliatelle. Sprinkle with half of the peas and half of the prosciutto. Top with half of the mozzarella. Repeat layers. Dot with butter. Bake in preheated 350°F oven 20 minutes or until heated through.   *Makes 4 to 6 servings*

Rigatoni with Sausage & Beans

Quick Pasta Puttanesca

1 package (16 ounces) uncooked spaghetti or linguine
3 tablespoons plus 1 teaspoon olive oil, divided
¼ to 1 teaspoon red pepper flakes
2 cans (6 ounces each) chunk light tuna packed in water, drained
1 tablespoon dried minced onion
1 teaspoon minced garlic
1 can (28 ounces) diced tomatoes
1 can (8 ounces) tomato sauce
24 pitted kalamata or black olives
2 tablespoons capers, drained

1. Cook spaghetti according to package directions; drain and return to saucepan. Add 1 teaspoon oil; toss to coat. Cover and keep warm.

2. Meanwhile, heat remaining 3 tablespoons oil in large skillet over medium-high heat. Add red pepper flakes; cook and stir 1 to 2 minutes or until sizzling. Add tuna; cook and stir 2 to 3 minutes. Add onion and garlic; cook and stir 1 minute. Add tomatoes, tomato sauce, olives and capers; cook and stir over medium-high heat until sauce is heated through.

3. Add sauce to spaghetti; mix well. *Makes 6 to 8 servings*

Quick Pasta Puttanesca

Asparagus-Parmesan Risotto

5½ cups chicken or vegetable broth
⅛ teaspoon salt
4 tablespoons unsalted butter, divided
⅓ cup finely chopped onion
2 cups uncooked arborio rice
⅔ cup dry white wine
2½ cups fresh asparagus, cut into 1-inch pieces
⅔ cup frozen peas
1 cup grated Parmesan cheese

1. Bring broth and salt to a boil in medium saucepan over medium-high heat; reduce heat to low and simmer.

2. Meanwhile, melt 3 tablespoons butter in large saucepan over medium heat. Add onion; cook and stir 2 to 3 minutes or until tender. Stir in rice; cook 2 minutes or until rice is coated with butter, stirring frequently. Add wine; cook, stirring occasionally, until most of wine is absorbed.

3. Add 1½ cups hot broth; cook and stir 6 to 7 minutes or until most of liquid is absorbed. (Mixture should simmer, but not boil.) Add 2 cups broth and asparagus; cook and stir 6 to 7 minutes or until most of liquid is absorbed. Add remaining 2 cups broth and peas; cook and stir 5 to 6 minutes or until most of liquid is absorbed and rice mixture is creamy.

4. Remove from heat; stir in remaining 1 tablespoon butter and Parmesan until melted. *Makes 4 servings*

Asparagus-Spinach Risotto: Substitute 1 cup baby spinach leaves or chopped large spinach leaves for peas. Proceed as directed.

Asparagus-Chicken Risotto: Add 2 cups chopped or shredded cooked chicken to risotto with peas in step 3. Proceed as directed.

Tip: The broth can be added in smaller increments of ½ to ¾ cup, if desired. Just be sure to stir the rice mixture constantly for a creamy texture.

Asparagus-Parmesan Risotto

Spicy Italian Sausage & Penne Pasta

8 ounces uncooked penne or tortiglioni pasta
1 pound bulk hot Italian sausage
1 cup chopped onion
2 cloves garlic, minced
2 cans (about 14 ounces each) seasoned diced tomatoes
3 cups broccoli florets
½ cup shredded Asiago or Romano cheese

1. Cook penne according to package directions; drain. Return to saucepan; keep warm.

2. Meanwhile, place sausage and onion in large skillet. Cook and stir until sausage is no longer pink, stirring to break up meat; drain fat. Add garlic; cook 1 minute. Stir in tomatoes and broccoli. Cover; cook 10 minutes or until broccoli is tender.

3. Add sausage mixture to penne; toss well. Sprinkle with Asiago.

Makes 4 to 6 servings

Tip: To add fabulous extra flavor to pasta dishes, slice fresh basil leaves into thin shreds. Sprinkle basil over pasta just before serving.

Linguine with Oil and Garlic

½ cup FILIPPO BERIO® Extra Virgin Olive Oil, divided
10 cloves garlic, minced
¾ pound uncooked linguine
¼ teaspoon black pepper
¼ teaspoon salt (optional)

1. Heat 2 tablespoons olive oil in small saucepan over medium heat. Add garlic; cook and stir until lightly browned. Remove from heat; set aside.

2. Cook linguine according to package directions until tender. Do not overcook.

3. Drain pasta; return to saucepan. Toss with garlic and olive oil mixture, remaining 6 tablespoons olive oil, pepper and salt, if desired.

Makes 4 servings

Spicy Italian Sausage & Penne Pasta

Baked Gnocchi

1 package (about 17 ounces) gnocchi
⅓ cup olive oil
3 cloves garlic, minced
1 package (10 ounces) frozen spinach, thawed and squeezed dry
1 can (about 14 ounces) diced tomatoes
1 teaspoon Italian seasoning
   Salt and black pepper
½ cup grated Parmesan cheese
½ cup (2 ounces) shredded mozzarella cheese

1. Preheat oven to 350°F. Grease large casserole or gratin dish.

2. Cook gnocchi according to package directions; drain.

3. Meanwhile, heat oil in large skillet or Dutch oven over medium heat. Add garlic; cook and stir 30 seconds. Stir in spinach; cook, covered, 2 minutes or until spinach wilts. Add tomatoes, Italian seasoning, salt and pepper; cook and stir about 5 minutes. Add gnocchi to spinach mixture; stir gently.

4. Transfer gnocchi mixture to prepared casserole. Sprinkle with Parmesan and mozzarella. Bake 20 to 30 minutes or until casserole is bubbly and cheese is melted.   *Makes 4 to 6 servings*

note

Gnocchi is the Italian word for dumplings. They are typically made from potatoes or flour, shaped into small balls and cooked in boiling water like pasta.

Baked Gnocchi

Spaghetti & Meatballs

¾ **pound ground beef**
¼ **pound spicy Italian sausage, casing removed**
 1 **egg white**
 2 **tablespoons plain dry bread crumbs**
 1 **teaspoon dried oregano**
 8 **ounces uncooked spaghetti**
 2 **cups prepared tomato-basil pasta sauce**
¼ **cup grated Parmesan cheese**
 2 **tablespoons chopped fresh basil**

1. Preheat oven to 450°F. Spray baking sheet with nonstick cooking spray.

2. Combine beef, sausage, egg white, bread crumbs and oregano in medium bowl; mix well. Shape mixture into 16 (1½-inch) meatballs. Place meatballs on prepared baking sheet; spray with cooking spray. Bake 12 minutes, turning once.

3. Meanwhile, cook spaghetti according to package directions.

4. Pour pasta sauce into large skillet; add meatballs. Cook and stir over medium heat about 9 minutes or until sauce is heated through and meatballs are no longer pink in center.

5. Drain spaghetti; divide among 4 plates. Top with meatballs and sauce; sprinkle with Parmesan and basil.   *Makes 4 servings*

Spaghetti & Meatballs

Wild Mushroom Risotto

1 cup sliced portobello mushrooms
1 cup sliced shiitake mushrooms, stems discarded
½ cup finely chopped onion
2 tablespoons *French's®* Worcestershire Sauce
2 cups uncooked arborio rice or white rice
2 cans (10½ ounces each) condensed chicken broth
½ cup frozen baby peas
½ cup (2 ounces) grated Parmesan cheese

1. Heat *1 tablespoon oil* in 5-quart saucepot or Dutch oven over medium-high heat. Add mushrooms and onion. Cook and stir 3 minutes or until mushrooms are tender. Add Worcestershire. Cook, stirring, until liquid is absorbed.

2. Add rice; cook 2 minutes, stirring constantly. Combine broth and *2½ cups water.* Add *4 cups* liquid to rice. Heat to boiling. Reduce heat to medium-low. Cook, uncovered, 8 minutes or until liquid is absorbed, stirring often. Add remaining broth, *½ cup* at a time. Cook and stir until rice is firm but tender and creamy.

3. Stir in peas and cheese; cook 1 minute. Serve with tossed green salad, if desired.   *Makes 4 servings*

Prep Time: 5 minutes
Cook Time: about 15 minutes

Classic Pasta Sauce

1 pound mild Italian sausage with fennel
½ cup chopped onion
2 cloves garlic, minced
1 can (28 ounces) tomato sauce
1 can (28 ounces) crushed tomatoes
¼ cup red wine (optional)
1 tablespoon chopped peperoncini
1 teaspoon dried oregano
½ teaspoon dried basil
   Hot cooked pasta
   Grated Parmesan cheese

1. Remove sausage from casings. Cook sausage, onion and garlic in large saucepan over medium-high heat until sausage is no longer pink, stirring to separate meat; drain fat.

2. Add tomato sauce, crushed tomatoes, wine, if desired, peperoncini, oregano and basil. Simmer over low heat about 30 minutes to blend flavors. Serve over pasta; sprinkle with Parmesan.   *Makes about 7 cups sauce*

Tip: This sauce freezes well. Keep on hand for a quick dinner on busy nights.

Sweet Sausage Fusilli

    2 tablespoons extra-virgin olive oil, divided
    12 ounces sweet Italian poultry sausage, sliced into ½-inch-thick half moons
    1½ teaspoons chopped fresh oregano
      Kosher salt and red pepper flakes to taste
    1 quart (8 ounces) broccoli florets, blanched
    1 cup California Ripe Olives, whole, pitted
    1 quart cooked fusilli pasta
    ¼ cup shaved Parmesan cheese

Heat 1 tablespoon olive oil in large skillet over medium-high heat. Stir in sausage and oregano, and season to taste with salt and pepper flakes. Cook for 3 to 5 minutes until browned. Mix in broccoli, California Ripe Olives and pasta and cook until heated through. Toss with remaining olive oil and top with Parmesan cheese just before serving.   *Makes 4 servings*

Favorite recipe from ***California Olive Industry***

Baked Ravioli with Pumpkin Sauce

1 package (9 ounces) refrigerated cheese ravioli
1 tablespoon butter
1 shallot, finely chopped
1 cup whipping cream
1 cup solid-pack pumpkin
½ cup shredded Asiago cheese, divided
½ teaspoon salt
¼ teaspoon ground nutmeg
⅛ teaspoon black pepper
½ cup coarse dry bread crumbs or small croutons

1. Preheat oven to 350°F. Grease 2-quart baking dish.

2. Cook ravioli according to package directions; drain.

3. Meanwhile, melt butter in medium saucepan. Add shallot; cook and stir over medium heat 3 minutes or until tender. Add cream, pumpkin, ¼ cup Asiago, salt, nutmeg and pepper; cook and stir over low heat 2 minutes or until cheese is melted. Gently stir in cooked ravioli.

4. Spoon ravioli and pumpkin sauce mixture into prepared baking dish. Combine remaining ¼ cup Asiago and croutons; sprinkle over ravioli.

5. Bake 15 minutes or until sauce is heated through and topping is lightly browned.   *Makes 4 servings*

Baked Ravioli with Pumpkin Sauce

Linguine with Herbs, Tomatoes and Capers

    1 package (9 ounces) refrigerated fresh linguine
    2 tablespoons olive oil
    2 cups chopped tomatoes
    2 cloves garlic, minced
    ¼ cup finely chopped green onions
    3 tablespoons capers
    2 tablespoons finely chopped fresh basil
    ¼ teaspoon salt
    ⅛ teaspoon black pepper
    ½ cup grated Parmesan cheese

1. Cook linguine according to package directions; drain.

2. Meanwhile, heat oil in large skillet over medium-high heat. Add tomatoes and garlic; cook 3 minutes or until tomatoes begin to break down and soften, stirring frequently. Stir in green onions, capers, basil, salt and pepper.

3. Add linguine to skillet; toss with tomato mixture. Sprinkle with Parmesan. *Makes 4 to 6 servings*

Gnocchi with BelGioioso® Gorgonzola

    2 pounds potatoes
  2⅓ cups all-purpose flour
    1 egg
      Salt to taste
    1 cup BELGIOIOSO® Gorgonzola Cheese
    1 tablespoon water
      Black pepper to taste

Boil and peel potatoes; mash. Add flour, egg and salt; mix by hand until dough is soft and compact. With floured hands, make small potato rolls (almost like dumplings). Drop into boiling water to cook. Meanwhile, cut BELGIOIOSO Gorgonzola into cubes; melt in pan over low heat. Add water and pepper. Toss cooked gnocchi with Gorgonzola sauce; serve. *Makes 6 servings*

Linguine with Herbs, Tomatoes and Capers

Veggie No Boiling Lasagna

1 tablespoon olive oil
1 medium sweet onion, thinly sliced
1 medium red bell pepper, thinly sliced
1 medium zucchini, cut in half lengthwise and thinly sliced
2 containers (15 ounces each) ricotta cheese
2 cups shredded mozzarella cheese (about 8 ounces), divided
½ cup grated Parmesan cheese, divided
2 eggs
2 jars (1 pound 10 ounces each) RAGÚ® Old World Style® Pasta Sauce
12 uncooked lasagna noodles

1. Preheat oven to 375°F. In 12-inch nonstick skillet, heat olive oil over medium-high heat and cook onion, red bell pepper and zucchini, stirring occasionally, 5 minutes or until softened.

2. Meanwhile, combine ricotta cheese, 1 cup mozzarella cheese, ¼ cup Parmesan cheese and eggs.

3. In 13×9-inch baking dish, spread 1 cup Pasta Sauce. Layer 4 uncooked noodles, then 1 cup Sauce, half of ricotta mixture and half of vegetables; repeat. Top with remaining uncooked noodles and 2 cups Sauce. Reserve remaining Sauce.

4. Cover with foil and bake 1 hour. Remove foil; sprinkle with remaining cheeses. Bake uncovered 10 minutes. Let stand 10 minutes before serving. Serve with reserved Pasta Sauce, heated.

Makes 12 servings

Prep Time: 15 minutes
Cook Time: 1 hour, 10 minutes

Veggie No Boiling Lasagna

Homemade Spinach Ravioli

1 package (10 ounces) frozen chopped spinach, thawed and
   squeezed dry
1 cup ricotta cheese
½ cup grated Romano or Parmesan cheese
1 egg
1 tablespoon minced fresh basil
½ teaspoon salt
½ teaspoon black pepper
¼ teaspoon ground nutmeg
36 wonton wrappers (thawed, if frozen)
1 jar (about 26 ounces) marinara or other pasta sauce

1. Combine spinach, ricotta, Romano, egg, basil, salt, pepper and
nutmeg in medium bowl. (Filling may be prepared up to 1 day in
advance and refrigerated.)

2. Place 1 or 2 wonton wrappers on lightly floured surface, keeping
remaining wrappers covered. Place 1 heaping teaspoon filling in
center of each wrapper. Moisten edges around filling and place
another wrapper on top; press edges gently around filling to remove
air bubbles and seal. (If using square wrappers, cut with 1½-inch
round or scalloped cookie cutter, if desired.) Repeat with remaining
wrappers. (Any leftover filling may be frozen for later use.)

3. Bring large saucepan of salted water to a boil. Meanwhile, heat
marinara sauce in medium saucepan over low heat. Add half of
ravioli to boiling water; reduce heat to medium-high. Stir gently and
cook until ravioli rise to top (about 3 minutes). Remove ravioli with
slotted spoon and keep warm. Repeat with remaining ravioli. Serve
with marinara sauce. *Makes 18 ravioli*

Homemade Spinach Ravioli

Manicotti

1 container (16 ounces) ricotta cheese
2 cups (8 ounces) shredded mozzarella cheese
½ cup cottage cheese
2 eggs, beaten
2 tablespoons grated Parmesan cheese
½ teaspoon minced garlic
   Salt and black pepper
1 package (about 8 ounces) uncooked manicotti shells
1 pound ground beef
1 jar (26 ounces) pasta sauce
2 cups water

1. Preheat oven to 375°F.

2. Combine ricotta, mozzarella, cottage cheese, eggs, Parmesan and garlic in large bowl; mix well. Season with salt and pepper. Fill manicotti shells with cheese mixture; place in 13×9-inch baking dish.

3. Brown beef in large skillet over medium-high heat, stirring to break up meat; drain fat. Stir in pasta sauce and water (mixture will be thin). Pour sauce over filled manicotti shells.

4. Cover with foil. Bake 1 hour or until sauce is thickened and shells are tender. *Makes 6 servings*

note

Manicotti shells are usually cooked before they are filled. This recipe eliminates that extra step by filling uncooked shells and adding water to the sauce—the shells cook in the liquid as the casserole is baking.

Manicotti

taste-tempting pizza & panini

Classic Potato, Onion & Ham Pizza

3 tablespoons butter or olive oil, divided
3 cups new potatoes, cut into ¼-inch slices
2 sweet onions, cut into ¼-inch slices
1 tablespoon coarsely chopped garlic
½ teaspoon salt
½ teaspoon black pepper
2 cups (8 ounces) shredded Wisconsin Mozzarella cheese
1 (16-ounce) Italian-style bread shell pizza crust
8 thin slices (4 ounces) deli ham
8 slices (4 ounces) Wisconsin Provolone cheese
⅓ cup grated Wisconsin Parmesan cheese
¼ cup chopped Italian parsley

Melt 2 tablespoons butter or olive oil in large skillet over medium heat; add potatoes, onions, garlic, salt and pepper. Cook 12 to 15 minutes, turning occasionally. Add remaining 1 tablespoon butter. Cook 5 to 7 minutes or until potatoes are golden brown. Cool slightly.

Preheat oven to 400°F. Sprinkle mozzarella cheese over crust; top with ham slices. Arrange potato mixture over ham; top with provolone cheese. Sprinkle with Parmesan cheese and parsley. Place crust directly on oven rack; bake for 15 to 20 minutes or until cheese is melted. *Makes 4 servings*

Favorite Recipe from **Wisconsin Milk Marketing Board**

Portobello Provolone Panini

  6 to 8 ounces sliced portobello mushrooms
  ⅓ cup plus 1 tablespoon olive oil, divided
  3 tablespoons balsamic vinegar
  1 clove garlic, minced
  ½ teaspoon salt
  ¼ teaspoon black pepper
  1 loaf (16 ounces) ciabatta or Italian bread *or* 4 ciabatta rolls
  8 ounces sliced provolone cheese
  ¼ cup chopped fresh basil
  8 ounces plum tomatoes, thinly sliced
  3 tablespoons whole-grain Dijon mustard

1. Place mushrooms, ⅓ cup oil, vinegar, garlic, salt and pepper in large resealable food storage bag. Seal tightly; shake to coat mushrooms evenly. Let stand 15 minutes, turning frequently. (Mushrooms may be prepared up to 24 hours in advance; refrigerate and turn occasionally.

2. Preheat indoor grill. Slice bread in half lengthwise; brush both sides of bread with remaining 1 tablespoon oil.

3. Arrange mushrooms evenly over bottom half of cut bread; drizzle with marinade. Top with provolone, basil and tomatoes. Spread mustard evenly over cut side of remaining half of bread. Place over tomatoes. Cut sandwich into 4 equal pieces.

4. Grill each sandwich 8 minutes or until bread is golden and cheese is melted. Wrap each sandwich tightly in foil to keep warm or serve at room temperature. *Makes 4 servings*

Portobello Provolone Panini

Italian Sausage and Bell Pepper Pizza

1 cup (½ of 15-ounce can) CONTADINA® Original Pizza Sauce
1 (12-inch) prepared pre-baked pizza crust
1 cup (4 ounces) shredded mozzarella cheese
½ cup (2 ounces) shredded Parmesan cheese
4 ounces (about 2 links) mild Italian sausage, cooked and sliced or crumbled
1 small green bell pepper, cut into thin strips

1. Spread pizza sauce onto crust to within 1 inch of edge.

2. Sprinkle with ½ cup mozzarella cheese, Parmesan cheese, sausage, bell pepper and remaining mozzarella cheese.

3. Bake according to pizza crust package directions or until crust is crisp and cheese is melted. *Makes 8 servings*

Chicken-Pesto Pizza

1 tablespoon olive oil
½ pound chicken tenders, cut into bite-size pieces
1 medium onion, thinly sliced
⅓ cup prepared pesto
3 medium plum tomatoes, thinly sliced
1 (14-inch) prepared pizza crust
1 cup (4 ounces) shredded mozzarella cheese

1. Preheat oven to 450°F. Heat oil in large skillet over medium heat. Add chicken; cook and stir 2 minutes. Add onion and pesto; cook and stir about 3 minutes or until chicken is cooked through.

2. Arrange tomato slices and chicken mixture on pizza crust to within 1 inch of edge. Sprinkle with mozzarella.

3. Bake 8 minutes or until pizza is heated through and cheese is melted and bubbly. *Makes 6 servings*

Italian Sausage and Bell Pepper Pizza

Panini with Fresh Mozzarella and Basil

½ **cup prepared vinaigrette**
1 **loaf (16 ounces) Italian bread, cut in half lengthwise**
6 **ounces fresh mozzarella cheese, cut into 12 slices**
8 **ounces thinly sliced oven-roasted deli turkey**
12 to 16 **fresh whole basil leaves**
1 **large tomato, thinly sliced**
½ **cup thinly sliced red onion**
⅛ **teaspoon red pepper flakes**

1. Preheat indoor grill. Spoon vinaigrette evenly over both cut sides of bread.

2. Arrange mozzarella evenly over bottom half of bread; top with turkey, basil, tomato and onion. Sprinkle with red pepper flakes. Cover with top half of bread; press down firmly. Cut into 4 sandwiches.

3. Grill sandwiches 5 to 7 minutes or until cheese is melted.

Makes 4 servings

Salami & Provolone Panini

8 **slices Italian or white bread**
12 **slices Genoa or hard salami**
8 **slices provolone cheese**
1 **cup arugula or baby spinach leaves**
¼ **cup HELLMANN'S® or BEST FOODS® Mayonnaise Dressing with Extra Virgin Olive Oil**

1. Evenly top 4 bread slices with salami, cheese and arugula, then remaining bread slices.

2. Brush both sides of sandwiches with HELLMANN'S® or BEST FOODS® Mayonnaise Dressing with Extra Virgin Olive Oil. In 12-inch skillet or grill pan, cook sandwiches over medium heat, turning once, 6 minutes or until bread is toasted and cheese is melted.

Makes 4 servings

Panini with Fresh Mozzarella and Basil

Simple Sausage Pizza

½ **cup tomato sauce**
1 **garlic clove, minced**
½ **teaspoon dried basil**
½ **teaspoon dried oregano**
⅛ **teaspoon red pepper flakes (optional)**
2 **grilled sausage links**
1 **grilled red onion**
1 **grilled bell pepper**
1 **(12-inch) prepared pizza crust**
1½ **cups (6 ounces) shredded fontina or pizza cheese blend**
½ **cup grated Parmesan cheese**

1. Preheat oven to 450°F. Combine tomato sauce, garlic, basil, oregano and red pepper flakes, if desired, in small bowl.

2. Cut sausages in half lengthwise, then cut crosswise into ½-inch slices. Cut onion and bell pepper into 1-inch pieces.

3. Place pizza crust on pizza pan or baking sheet. Spread tomato sauce mixture over crust to within 1 inch of edge. Sprinkle fontina over tomato sauce; top with sausage, onion and bell pepper. Sprinkle with Parmesan.

4. Bake about 12 minutes or until crust is crisp and cheese is melted.

Makes 4 servings

Tip: To save time, ½ cup prepared pizza sauce may be substituted for the tomato sauce and seasonings.

Simple Sausage Pizza

Pizza Sandwich

1 loaf (12 ounces) focaccia
½ cup pizza sauce
20 slices pepperoni
8 slices (1 ounce each) mozzarella cheese
1 can (2¼ ounces) sliced mushrooms, drained
Red pepper flakes (optional)
Olive oil

1. Cut focaccia horizontally in half. Spread cut sides of both halves with pizza sauce. Layer bottom half with pepperoni, mozzarella and mushrooms; sprinkle with red pepper flakes, if desired. Cover with top half of focaccia. Brush sandwich lightly with olive oil.

2. Heat large nonstick skillet over medium heat. Add sandwich; press down lightly with spatula or weigh down with small plate. Cook sandwich 4 to 5 minutes per side or until cheese is melted and sandwich is golden brown. Cut into wedges.

Makes 4 to 6 servings

Note: Focaccia can be found in the bakery section of most supermarkets. It is often available in different flavors, such as tomato, herb, cheese or onion.

Plum Tomato Basil Pizza

1 cup (4 ounces) shredded mozzarella cheese
1 (10-ounce) package prepared pizza crust
4 ripe seeded Italian plum tomatoes, sliced
½ cup fresh basil leaves
1½ teaspoons Original TABASCO® brand Pepper Sauce
Olive oil

Preheat oven to 425°F. Sprinkle shredded mozzarella cheese evenly over pizza crust. Layer with tomatoes and basil. Drizzle with TABASCO® Sauce and olive oil. Bake on pizza pan or stone 15 minutes or until cheese is melted and crust is golden brown.

Makes 4 servings

Pizza Sandwich

Mozzarella-Prosciutto Panini

1 BAYS® English Muffin, split
½ teaspoon bottled Italian dressing
¼ ounce prosciutto
   Thinly sliced Roma tomato
1½ ounces smoked mozzarella, sliced to fit inside of muffin
1 teaspoon softened butter

Preheat heavy skillet or griddle over low heat until spatter of water disappears quickly. Sprinkle each half of muffin with Italian dressing. Layer prosciutto, tomato and smoked mozzarella on bottom of muffin. Replace top. Spread softened butter on outside of sandwich.

Place sandwich bottom side down in preheated skillet. Place heavy saucepan weighted with 2 cans or brick wrapped in heavy duty foil on top to flatten panini. Cook 3 minutes. Turn and cook on second side 3 minutes with weight in place until cheese starts to sizzle into pan. Remove weight and finish cooking.   *Makes 1 serving*

Turkey Cheddar Panini: For each panini, spread inside of bottom half of muffin with 2 teaspoons chutney; top with ½ ounce sliced turkey and 1 ounce Cheddar cheese. Spread 1 teaspoon softened butter on outside of sandwich. Cook 3 minutes per side as directed above.

Fontina-Caponata Panini: For each panini, spread inside of bottom half of muffin with 1 rounded tablespoonful of prepared caponata (eggplant appetizer); top with 1½ ounces fontina sliced to fit muffin. Spread 1 teaspoon softened butter on outside of sandwich. Cook 3 minutes per side as directed above.

Pizza Bianca

2 tablespoons olive oil, plus more to brush baking sheet
1 pound white or whole-wheat pizza dough
2 teaspoons minced garlic
2 cups grated CABOT® Sharp Cheddar (about 8 ounces)
2 tablespoons coarsely chopped fresh rosemary leaves *or* ¼ cup torn fresh basil leaves

1. Place rack in lower third of oven and preheat oven to 450°F. Brush large baking sheet generously with oil.

2. On floured work surface, roll dough out into rectangle the size of baking sheet, letting it rest for several minutes if it becomes too springy to work with. Transfer to prepared baking sheet.

3. In small skillet, heat oil over medium heat; add garlic and cook, stirring, until garlic is fragrant and just beginning to color, about 1 minute. Immediately brush mixture all over top of dough.

4. Sprinkle with cheese and scatter rosemary or basil on top. Bake for 12 to 15 minutes, or until golden on top and browned underneath. Serve hot or at room temperature.

Makes 4 servings

Panini with Prosciutto, Mozzarella and Ripe Olives

   1 cup California Ripe Olives, sliced
  ¼ cup chopped fresh basil
   8 wedges prepared herb focaccia
  ⅓ cup coarse mustard
   1 pound prosciutto, sliced
24 ounces mozzarella, thinly sliced
   4 cups arugula, washed, dried

Combine sliced olives and basil in bowl; mix well. Slice each focaccia wedge horizontally in half. Spread cut sides of each wedge with 1 teaspoon mustard. Layer bottom halves with 2 tablespoons olive mixture, 2 ounces prosciutto, 3 ounces mozzarella and ½ cup arugula. Top with remaining focaccia halves.

Makes 8 servings

Favorite recipe from **California Olive Industry**

Caprese Pizza

1 loaf (1 pound) frozen pizza or bread dough, thawed
1 container (12 ounces) bruschetta sauce
1 container (8 ounces) pearl-sized fresh mozzarella (perlini), drained*

*If pearl-size mozzarella is not available, use one 8-ounce ball of fresh mozzarella and chop into ¼-inch pieces.

1. Preheat oven to 400°F. Spray jelly-roll pan or baking sheet with nonstick cooking spray.

2. Roll out dough on lightly floured surface to 15×10-inch rectangle. Transfer to prepared pan. Cover loosely with plastic wrap; let rest 10 minutes. Meanwhile, drain bruschetta sauce 10 minutes.

3. Prick surface of dough several times with fork; bake 10 minutes. Sprinkle with bruschetta sauce and top with mozzarella. Bake 10 minutes or until cheese is melted and crust is golden brown. Serve warm. *Makes 6 servings*

Bruschetta sauce is a mixture of fresh tomatoes, garlic, basil and olive oil. It is usually found in the refrigerated section of the supermarket with other prepared dips such as hummus.

Caprese Pizza

Portobello & Fontina Sandwiches

2 teaspoons olive oil
2 large portobello mushrooms, stems removed
   Salt and black pepper
2 to 3 tablespoons sun-dried tomato pesto
4 slices crusty Italian bread
4 ounces fontina cheese, sliced
½ cup fresh basil leaves
   Additional olive oil

1. Preheat broiler. Line baking sheet with foil.

2. Drizzle 2 teaspoons oil over both sides of mushrooms; season with salt and pepper. Place mushrooms, gill sides up, on prepared baking sheet. Broil mushrooms 4 minutes per side or until tender. Cut into ¼-inch-thick slices.

3. Spread pesto evenly on 2 bread slices; layer with mushrooms, fontina and basil. Top with remaining bread slices. Brush outsides of sandwiches lightly with additional oil.

4. Heat large grill pan or skillet over medium heat. Add sandwiches; press down lightly with spatula or weigh down with small plate. Cook sandwiches 4 to 5 minutes per side or until cheese is melted and sandwiches are golden brown.   *Makes 2 sandwiches*

Portobello & Fontina Sandwich

Caramelized Onion and Olive Pizza

2 tablespoons olive oil

1½ pounds onions, thinly sliced

2 teaspoons fresh rosemary leaves *or* 1 teaspoon dried rosemary

¼ cup water

1 tablespoon balsamic vinegar

1 cup California Ripe Olives, sliced

1 (12-inch) prebaked thick pizza crust

2 cups (8 ounces) shredded mozzarella cheese

Heat oil in medium nonstick skillet. Add onions and rosemary. Cook, stirring frequently, until onions begin to brown and browned bits begin to stick to bottom of skillet, about 15 minutes. Stir in ¼ cup water; scrape up any browned bits. Reduce heat to medium-low and continue to cook, stirring occasionally, until onions are golden and sweet-tasting, 15 to 30 minutes; add more water, 1 tablespoon at a time, if onion mixture appears dry. Remove pan from heat and stir in vinegar, scraping up any browned bits from pan. Gently stir in olives. Place crust on pizza pan or baking sheet. Spoon onion mixture into center of crust. Sprinkle with cheese. Bake in 450°F oven until cheese is melted and just beginning to brown, about 15 minutes. Cut into wedges and serve warm.

Makes 8 to 10 servings

Prep Time: 15 minutes
Cook Time: about 1 hour

Favorite recipe from *California Olive Industry*

Caramelized Onion and Olive Pizza

Spinach & Roasted Pepper Panini

    1 loaf (12 ounces) focaccia
1½ cups spinach leaves
    1 jar (about 7 ounces) roasted red peppers, drained
    4 ounces fontina cheese, thinly sliced
  ¾ cup thinly sliced red onion
     Olive oil

1. Cut focaccia horizontally in half. Layer bottom half with spinach, peppers, fontina and onion. Cover with top half of focaccia. Brush outsides of sandwich very lightly with oil. Cut sandwich into 4 equal pieces.

2. Heat large nonstick skillet over medium heat. Add sandwiches; press down lightly with spatula or weigh down with small plate. Cook sandwiches 4 to 5 minutes per side or until cheese is melted and sandwiches are golden brown. *Makes 4 servings*

Quattro Formaggio Pizza

  ½ cup prepared pizza or marinara sauce
  1 (12-inch) prepared pizza crust
  4 ounces shaved or thinly sliced provolone cheese
  2 ounces Asiago or brick cheese, thinly sliced
  1 cup (4 ounces) shredded smoked or regular mozzarella cheese
  ¼ cup grated Parmesan or Romano cheese

1. Preheat oven to 450°F. Spread pizza sauce evenly over pizza crust; place on baking sheet.

2. Sprinkle with provolone and Asiago; top with mozzarella and Parmesan. Bake 14 minutes or until pizza crust is golden brown and cheeses are melted. Cut into wedges; serve immediately.
Makes 4 servings

Spinach & Roasted Pepper Panini

Stuffed Pizza

2 loaves (1 pound each) frozen bread dough, thawed
1 bottle (15 ounces) CONTADINA® Pizza Squeeze Pizza Sauce, divided
1 package (3 ounces) sliced pepperoni, quartered
1 package (10 ounces) frozen chopped spinach, thawed and squeezed dry
1 cup (4 ounces) shredded mozzarella cheese
1 carton (8 ounces) ricotta cheese
1 cup grated Parmesan cheese
1 can (3.8 ounces) sliced ripe olives, drained
1 tablespoon olive oil
1 tablespoon grated Parmesan cheese

1. Roll bread dough into two 12-inch circles on floured surface. Place one circle on greased baking sheet.

2. Spread with ¼ cup pizza sauce to 1 inch from edge.

3. Combine pepperoni, spinach, mozzarella, ricotta, 1 cup Parmesan cheese and olives in large bowl. Spread mixture over pizza sauce. Squeeze ¼ cup pizza sauce evenly over filling; dampen outside edge. Place remaining bread dough on top and seal. Cut 8 steam vents.

4. Bake on lowest rack in preheated 350°F oven for 20 minutes. Brush with olive oil; sprinkle with 1 tablespoon Parmesan cheese.

5. Bake for additional 15 to 20 minutes or until well browned. Let stand 15 minutes before cutting. Warm remaining pizza sauce and serve over wedges of pizza.   *Makes 8 servings*

Prep Time: 20 minutes
Cook Time: 40 minutes
Stand Time: 15 minutes

Stuffed Pizza

exceptional entrées

Beef Spiedini with Orzo

¼ cup olive oil
¼ cup dry red wine
2 cloves garlic, minced
1 teaspoon dried rosemary
½ teaspoon coarse salt
½ teaspoon dried thyme
½ teaspoon coarsely ground black pepper
1½ pounds beef top sirloin steak, cut into 1 × 1¼-inch pieces
6 cups water
½ teaspoon salt
1 cup uncooked orzo
1 tablespoon butter
1 tablespoon chopped parsley
Fresh rosemary sprigs (optional)

1. Combine oil, wine, garlic, dried rosemary, coarse salt, thyme and pepper in large resealable food storage bag. Add beef; turn to coat. Marinate in refrigerator 15 to 30 minutes.

2. Prepare grill for direct cooking. Soak 8 (6- to 8-inch) wooden skewers in water 15 minutes.

3. Bring 6 cups water and salt to a boil in small saucepan over high heat. Add orzo; reduce heat and simmer 15 minutes or until tender. Drain. Stir in butter and parsley; keep warm.

4. Thread beef onto skewers. Grill over medium-high heat 8 to 10 minutes, turning occasionally. Serve with orzo. Garnish skewers with fresh rosemary.   *Makes 4 servings*

Pollo Diavolo (Deviled Chicken)

8 skinless bone-in chicken thighs (2½ to 3 pounds)
¼ cup olive oil
3 tablespoons lemon juice
6 cloves garlic, minced
1 to 2 teaspoons red pepper flakes
3 tablespoons butter, softened
1 teaspoon dried sage
1 teaspoon dried thyme
¾ teaspoon coarse salt
¼ teaspoon ground red pepper or black pepper
Lemon wedges

1. Place chicken in large resealable food storage bag. Combine oil, lemon juice, garlic and red pepper flakes in small bowl. Pour mixture over chicken. Seal bag; turn to coat. Refrigerate at least 1 hour or up to 8 hours, turning once.

2. Prepare grill for direct cooking. Drain chicken; reserve marinade. Place chicken on grid over medium-high heat; brush with reserved marinade. Grill, covered, 8 minutes. Turn chicken; brush with remaining marinade. Grill, covered, 8 to 10 minutes or until internal temperature reaches 165°F.

3. Meanwhile, combine butter, sage, thyme, salt and ground red pepper; mix well. Transfer chicken to serving platter; spread herb butter over chicken. Serve with lemon. *Makes 4 to 6 servings*

Pollo Diavolo (Deviled Chicken)

Grilled Steak with Arugula & Gorgonzola Salad

4 boneless beef top loin (strip) steaks (¾ inch thick)
1 cup balsamic or red wine vinaigrette, divided
2 cups mixed salad greens
1½ cups baby arugula leaves
½ cup crumbled Gorgonzola cheese

1. Combine steaks and ½ cup vinaigrette in large resealable food storage bag. Seal bag; turn to coat. Marinate in refrigerator 20 to 30 minutes. Meanwhile, prepare grill for direct cooking.

2. Remove steaks from marinade; discard marinade. Place steaks on grid over medium-high heat. Grill, covered, 6 to 8 minutes for medium-rare (145°F) or until desired doneness, turning once.

3. Meanwhile, combine salad greens and arugula in medium bowl. Pour remaining ½ cup vinaigrette over greens; toss until well coated. Serve steaks with salad. Sprinkle with Gorgonzola.

Makes 4 servings

Tuscan Lamb Skillet

8 lamb rib chops (1½ pounds), cut 1 inch thick
1 tablespoon olive oil
1 tablespoon minced garlic
1 can (about 19 ounces) cannellini beans, rinsed and drained
1 can (8 ounces) Italian-style tomatoes, undrained
1 tablespoon balsamic vinegar
2 teaspoons minced fresh rosemary leaves

1. Trim fat from lamb chops. Cook chops in oil in large skillet over medium heat 8 minutes or until thermometer inserted into center of chops registers 160°F for medium doneness, turning once. Transfer lamb chops to large plate; keep warm.

2. Add garlic to skillet; cook and stir 1 minute. Stir in beans, tomatoes with liquid, vinegar and rosemary. Bring to a boil; reduce heat to low. Simmer, uncovered, 5 minutes. Serve bean mixture with lamb chops.

Makes 4 servings

Grilled Steak with Arugula & Gorgonzola Salad

Tuna with Tomatoes & Olives

     2 tablespoons olive oil, divided
     1 small onion, quartered and sliced
     1 clove garlic, minced
  1⅓ cups chopped tomatoes
     ¼ cup sliced drained black olives
     2 anchovy fillets, finely chopped (optional)
     2 tablespoons chopped fresh basil
     ½ teaspoon salt, divided
     ⅛ teaspoon red pepper flakes
     4 tuna steaks (about 6 ounces each and cut ¾ inch thick)
        Black pepper
     ¼ cup toasted pine nuts

1. Heat 1 tablespoon oil in large skillet over medium heat. Add onion; cook and stir 4 minutes. Add garlic; cook and stir about 30 seconds. Add tomatoes; cook 3 minutes, stirring occasionally. Stir in olives, anchovies, if desired, basil, ¼ teaspoon salt and red pepper flakes. Cook until most of liquid is evaporated.

2. Meanwhile, sprinkle tuna with remaining ¼ teaspoon salt and black pepper. Heat remaining 1 tablespoon oil in large nonstick skillet over medium-high heat. Cook tuna 2 minutes on each side or until medium-rare. Serve with tomato mixture. Sprinkle with pine nuts.

Makes 4 servings

Tuna with Tomatoes & Olives

Tuscan Pork Loin Roast with Fig Sauce

   2 tablespoons olive oil
   3 cloves garlic, minced
   2 teaspoons coarse salt
   2 teaspoons dried rosemary
   ½ teaspoon red pepper flakes *or* 1 teaspoon black pepper
   1 center cut boneless pork loin roast (about 3 pounds)
   ¼ cup dry red wine
   1 jar (about 8 ounces) dried fig spread

1. Preheat oven to 350°F. Combine oil, garlic, salt, rosemary and red pepper flakes; brush over roast. Place roast on rack in shallow roasting pan.

2. Roast 1 hour or until internal temperature reaches 155°F. Transfer roast to carving board. Tent with foil; let stand 10 minutes. Cut roast into thin slices.

3. To deglaze, pour wine into roasting pan. Cook over medium-high heat, scraping up any browned bits and stirring frequently. Stir in fig spread. Cook and stir until melted and warm. Serve with pork.

Makes 6 to 8 servings

Roast Chicken Balsamic

   1 PERDUE® OVEN STUFFER® Roaster
   4 red onions, cut into wedges
   1 cup balsamic vinaigrette
   ½ cup chicken broth
   2 tablespoons chopped fresh Italian parsley

Preheat oven to 350°F. Set chicken in roasting dish and arrange onions around it. Pour vinaigrette and broth over chicken and onions. Roast until BIRD-WATCHER® Thermometer pops up and meat thermometer inserted into thickest part of thigh registers 180°F (approximately 2 hours).

Let chicken rest 10 minutes before carving. Serve with onions and sprinkle with parsley.

Makes 6 servings

Tuscan Pork Loin Roast with Fig Sauce

Spinach, Cheese and Prosciutto-Stuffed Chicken Breasts

4 boneless skinless chicken breasts (about 4 ounces each)
  Salt and black pepper
4 slices (½ ounce each) prosciutto*
4 slices (½ ounce each) smoked provolone**
1 cup spinach leaves, chopped
4 tablespoons all-purpose flour, divided
1 tablespoon olive oil
1 tablespoon butter
1 cup chicken broth
1 tablespoon whipping cream

Thinly sliced deli ham can be substituted for the prosciutto.

**Swiss, Gruyère or mozzarella cheese may be substituted for the smoked provolone.*

1. Preheat oven to 350°F.

2. Cut each chicken breast horizontally almost to opposite edge to form pocket. Fold back top half of chicken breast; sprinkle chicken lightly with salt and pepper. Place 1 slice prosciutto, 1 slice provolone and ¼ cup spinach on each chicken breast. Fold top half of breast over filling.

3. Lightly sprinkle chicken with salt and pepper. Spread 3 tablespoons flour on plate. Holding chicken breast closed, coat with flour; shake off excess.

4. Heat oil and butter in large skillet over medium heat. Place chicken in skillet; cook 4 minutes on each side or until browned.

5. Transfer chicken to shallow baking dish. Do not wash skillet; reserve to make sauce. Bake 10 minutes or until chicken is no longer pink in center.

6. Whisk chicken broth and cream into remaining 1 tablespoon flour in small bowl. Pour chicken broth mixture into reserved skillet; heat 3 minutes over medium heat, stirring constantly, until sauce thickens. Spoon sauce onto serving plates; top with chicken breasts.

Makes 4 servings

Spinach, Cheese and Prosciutto-Stuffed Chicken Breast

Italian Beef Ragu

2 tablespoons olive oil
1 cup chopped onion
2 cans (about 14 ounces each) fire-roasted diced tomatoes
1 teaspoon dried oregano
1 teaspoon dried basil
⅛ teaspoon red pepper flakes or black pepper
1 package (about 17 ounces) fully cooked beef pot roast (see Note)
8 ounces uncooked fettuccine

1. Heat oil in large saucepan over medium heat. Add onion; cook and stir 5 minutes or until translucent and slightly browned, stirring occasionally. Add tomatoes, oregano, basil and red pepper flakes; bring to a boil over high heat. Reduce heat; simmer, uncovered, 10 minutes, stirring occasionally.

2. Remove pot roast from package; add au jus to tomato mixture. Break meat into 1- to 1½-inch pieces. Add to tomato mixture; simmer 5 to 10 minutes or until heated through.

3. Meanwhile, cook fettuccine according to package directions; drain. Divide fettuccine among 4 serving plates; top with beef ragu.

Makes 4 servings

Fully cooked beef pot roast can be found in the refrigerated prepared meats section of the supermarket.

Italian Beef Ragu

Chicken Tuscany

6 medium red potatoes, scrubbed and sliced ⅛ inch thick

12 ounces shiitake, cremini, chanterelle and/or button mushrooms, sliced

4 tablespoons olive oil, divided

4 tablespoons grated Parmesan cheese, divided

3 teaspoons minced garlic, divided

3 teaspoons minced fresh rosemary leaves *or* 1½ teaspoons dried rosemary leaves, divided

Salt and ground black pepper

1 package (about 3 pounds) PERDUE® Fresh Pick of the Chicken

Preheat oven to 425°F. Pat potatoes dry with paper towels. Toss potatoes and mushrooms with 2½ tablespoons oil, 2 tablespoons cheese, 2 teaspoons garlic, 2 teaspoons rosemary, ½ teaspoon salt and ¼ teaspoon pepper. In 13×9-inch baking dish, arrange potatoes and mushrooms in one layer; top with remaining 2 tablespoons cheese. Bake 15 minutes or until potatoes are lightly browned; set aside.

Meanwhile, in large nonstick skillet over medium heat, heat remaining 1½ tablespoons oil. Add chicken pieces. Season lightly with salt and pepper; sprinkle with remaining 1 teaspoon rosemary and garlic. Cook chicken 5 to 6 minutes on each side or until browned. (Do not crowd pan; if necessary, brown chicken in two batches.)

Arrange chicken on top of potato mixture; drizzle with oil from skillet and return to oven. Bake 20 to 25 minutes longer or until chicken is no longer pink in center. Serve chicken, potatoes and mushrooms with green salad, if desired. *Makes 6 servings*

Chicken Tuscany

Prosciutto-Wrapped Snapper

1 tablespoon plus 1 teaspoon olive oil, divided
2 cloves garlic, minced
4 skinless red snapper fillets or halibut (about 6 to 7 ounces each)
½ teaspoon salt
½ teaspoon black pepper
8 large fresh sage leaves
8 thin slices prosciutto (4 ounces)
¼ cup dry Marsala wine

1. Preheat oven to 400°F.

2. Combine 1 tablespoon oil and garlic; brush over fish fillets. Sprinkle with salt and pepper. Lay two sage leaves on each fish fillet. Wrap two slices prosciutto around each fillet to enclose sage leaves and most of the fish. Tuck in ends of prosciutto.

3. Heat remaining 1 teaspoon oil in large ovenproof skillet over medium-high heat. Add fillets, top sides down; cook 3 to 4 minutes or until prosciutto is crisp. Carefully turn fish. Transfer skillet to oven; bake 8 to 10 minutes or until fish is opaque in center.

4. Transfer fish to serving plates; keep warm. To deglaze, pour wine into skillet. Cook over medium-high heat, scraping up browned bits. Stir constantly 2 to 3 minutes or until mixture has reduced by half. Drizzle over fish.

Makes 4 servings

Prosciutto-Wrapped Snapper

Mediterranean Chicken Thighs with Polenta

8 chicken thighs, skin and fat removed
½ teaspoon salt
¼ teaspoon pepper
3 teaspoons olive oil, divided
2 cloves garlic, minced
1 can (about 14 ounces) diced tomatoes
½ cup small pitted black olives, halved
1 teaspoon balsamic vinegar
2 bay leaves
1 can (about 15 ounces) cannellini beans, rinsed and drained
Polenta (recipe follows)
3 tablespoons chopped fresh parsley

1. Season chicken with salt and pepper. Heat 2 teaspoons oil in large nonstick skillet over medium heat. Add chicken; cook about 10 minutes or until browned, turning occasionally. Remove chicken; set aside.

2. Add remaining 1 teaspoon oil and garlic to skillet. Cook and stir 1 minute. Add tomatoes, olives, vinegar and bay leaves. Return chicken to pan. Cover; reduce heat to medium-low. Cook about 20 minutes or until chicken is fork-tender. Stir in beans; heat through. Remove bay leaves; discard.

3. Serve over polenta. Sprinkle with parsley.   *Makes 4 servings*

Polenta: Place 2½ cups water and ½ teaspoon salt in medium saucepan. Whisk in ¾ cup cornmeal. Cook over medium heat until mixture thickens, stirring occasionally. Stir in ½ cup grated Parmesan cheese.

Favorite recipe from **Delmarva Poultry Industry, Inc.**

Turkey Picatta

3 tablespoons all-purpose flour
¼ teaspoon salt
¼ teaspoon black pepper
2 egg whites
1 teaspoon water
⅔ cup plain dry bread crumbs
1 package (about 17½ ounces) turkey breast cutlets or slices
3 teaspoons butter, divided
3 teaspoons olive oil, divided
2 cloves garlic, minced
1 cup reduced-sodium chicken broth
2 tablespoons capers, rinsed and drained
2 tablespoons lemon juice
2 tablespoons chopped fresh parsley
1 teaspoon grated lemon peel

1. Preheat oven to 200°F. Combine flour, salt and pepper in small resealable food storage bag. Beat egg whites and water in small shallow bowl. Place bread crumbs in small shallow plate. Add 1 cutlet to bag; shake to coat lightly with flour mixture. Dip cutlet in egg mixture; let excess drip off. Press each side in bread crumbs. Repeat with remaining cutlets. Discard any remaining flour, egg whites or crumb mixture.

2. Heat 1 teaspoon butter and 1 teaspoon oil in large nonstick skillet over medium heat. Add half the cutlets; cook about 3 minutes on each side or until golden brown and no longer pink in center. Transfer cutlets to ovenproof serving plate; keep warm. Repeat with 1 teaspoon butter, 1 teaspoon oil and remaining cutlets. Transfer to serving plate in oven.

3. Heat remaining 1 teaspoon butter and 1 teaspoon oil in same skillet. Add garlic; cook 1 minute. Stir in broth, capers and lemon juice; simmer 1 to 2 minutes or until sauce is slightly reduced. Pour over turkey cutlets; top with parsley and lemon peel.

Makes 4 servings

Primavera Sauce with Artichokes and Shrimp

2 tablespoons olive oil
1 cup diced carrots
1 cup diced celery
1 small onion, diced
3 cloves garlic, finely chopped
1 can (28 ounces) CONTADINA® Recipe Ready Crushed Tomatoes with Italian Herbs
½ teaspoon salt
¼ teaspoon black pepper
8 ounces medium raw shrimp, peeled and deveined
1 cup sliced artichoke hearts, drained
Fresh chopped basil (optional)

1. Heat oil in large skillet over high heat. Add carrots, celery, onion and garlic. Cook for 4 to 5 minutes or until carrots are crisp-tender.

2. Add crushed tomatoes, salt and pepper. Bring to boil. Add shrimp and artichoke hearts. Cook for 2 to 3 minutes or until shrimp turn pink.

3. Reduce heat to low; simmer for 2 minutes to blend flavors. Sprinkle with basil. Serve over hot cooked pasta or rice, if desired.

Makes 6 servings

Prep Time: 12 minutes
Cook Time: 12 minutes

Primavera Sauce with Artichokes and Shrimp

Italian Sausage and Arugula Frittatas

  1 tablespoon olive oil
  2 links sweet Italian turkey sausage
  2 tablespoons finely chopped red onion
12 cremini mushrooms, sliced
  1 cup chopped arugula
¼ cup diced roasted red peppers
  8 eggs
½ teaspoon salt
¼ teaspoon black pepper
¼ cup shredded Italian cheese blend

1. Preheat oven to 350°F. Spray 4 (6-ounce) ramekins or custard cups with nonstick cooking spray; place on baking sheet.

2. Heat oil in medium skillet over medium heat. Remove sausage from casings; add to skillet. Cook until almost browned, stirring to break up sausage. Add onion; cook and stir 1 minute or until softened. Add mushrooms; cook and stir 5 minutes. Stir in arugula and roasted peppers; cook and stir 1 minute or until heated through. Divide mixture evenly among prepared ramekins.

3. Beat eggs, salt and black pepper in medium bowl until well blended. Pour over sausage mixture; sprinkle with cheese.

4. Bake 25 to 30 minutes or until centers are set. Cool 10 minutes; frittatas will deflate slightly. Serve warm or at room temperature.

Makes 4 servings

Italian Sausage and Arugula Frittata

Grilled Swordfish Sicilian Style

        3 tablespoons extra-virgin olive oil, plus additional for grid
        1 clove garlic, minced
        2 tablespoons lemon juice
        ¾ teaspoon salt
        ⅛ teaspoon black pepper
        3 tablespoons capers, drained
        1 tablespoon chopped fresh oregano or basil
    1½ pounds swordfish steaks (¾ inch thick)

1. Oil grid. Prepare grill for direct cooking. Heat 3 tablespoons oil in small saucepan over low heat. Add garlic; cook 1 minute. Remove from heat; cool slightly. Whisk in lemon juice, salt and pepper until salt is dissolved. Stir in capers and oregano.

2. Grill swordfish over medium heat 7 to 8 minutes, turning once, or until opaque in center. Serve with sauce.   *Makes 4 to 6 servings*

Veal Piccata

        1 pound veal cutlets (or chicken)
        2 cloves garlic, crushed
          All-purpose flour
        2 tablespoons oil
        4 tablespoons butter, divided
        ½ cup HOLLAND HOUSE® Vermouth Cooking Wine
        2 tablespoons lemon juice
        1 tablespoon chopped fresh parsley
          Freshly ground pepper

1. Rub veal or chicken with garlic; coat with flour. Heat oil and 2 tablespoons butter in large skillet over medium heat. Add veal or chicken; brown on both sides until cooked through. Transfer to serving platter; keep warm.

2. In small saucepan, combine cooking wine, remaining 2 tablespoons butter, lemon juice, parsley and pepper. Bring to a boil, stirring constantly. Cook 1 minute over high heat. Pour sauce over veal or chicken.   *Makes 4 servings*

Grilled Swordfish Sicilian Style

Italian Country-Style Braised Chicken

¾ **cup boiling water**
½ **cup dried porcini mushrooms (about ½ ounce)**
¼ **cup all-purpose flour**
1 **teaspoon salt**
½ **teaspoon black pepper**
1 **chicken, cut up (3½ to 4 pounds)**
3 **tablespoons olive oil**
2 **ounces pancetta or bacon, chopped**
1 **medium onion, chopped**
2 **carrots, thinly sliced**
3 **cloves garlic, minced**
1 **cup chicken broth**
1 **tablespoon tomato paste**
1 **cup green Italian olives**

1. Combine boiling water and mushrooms in small bowl. Let stand 15 to 20 minutes or until mushrooms are softened.

2. Meanwhile, combine flour, salt and pepper in large resealable food storage bag. Add 1 or 2 pieces of chicken at a time; toss to coat with flour. Discard any remaining flour mixture.

3. Heat oil in large skillet over medium heat. Brown chicken on both sides about 15 minutes or until golden brown. Transfer chicken to plate; set aside.

4. Pour off all but 1 tablespoon oil from skillet. Add pancetta, onion and carrots; cook 5 minutes, stirring occasionally to scrape up browned bits. Add garlic; cook 1 minute. Strain mushrooms, reserving liquid. Chop mushrooms. Add mushrooms and reserved liquid to skillet. Add broth and tomato paste; bring to a boil over high heat.

5. Return chicken to skillet with any juices from plate. Reduce heat; simmer, uncovered, 20 minutes or until chicken is cooked through and sauce thickens, turning once. Stir in olives; heat through. Transfer chicken to serving platter; top with sauce.

Makes 4 to 6 servings

Italian Country-Style Braised Chicken

Steak al Forno

4 cloves garlic, minced
1 tablespoon coarse salt
1 tablespoon olive oil
1 teaspoon black pepper
2 porterhouse or T-bone steaks (about 1 to 1¼ inches thick)
¼ cup grated Parmesan cheese

1. Prepare grill for direct cooking. Combine garlic, salt, oil and pepper; press into both sides of steaks. Let stand 15 minutes.

2. Place steaks on grid over medium-high heat. Cover; grill 14 to 19 minutes or until internal temperature reaches 145°F for medium-rare, turning once. Sprinkle Parmesan over steaks during last minute of cooking.

3. Transfer steaks to carving board; tent with foil. Let stand 5 minutes. To serve, cut meat away from each side of bone. Cut boneless pieces into slices. Serve immediately.

Makes 2 to 3 servings

Tip: For a smoked flavor, soak 2 cups hickory or oak wood chips in cold water to cover at least 30 minutes. Drain and scatter over hot coals before grilling.

Chicken Marsala

1 tablespoon butter
2 boneless skinless chicken breasts, halved
1 cup sliced carrots
1 cup sliced fresh mushrooms
⅓ cup chicken broth
⅓ cup HOLLAND HOUSE® Marsala Cooking Wine

Melt butter in skillet over medium-high heat. Add chicken; cook 5 minutes. Turn chicken over; add remaining ingredients. Bring to a boil; simmer 15 to 20 minutes until juices run clear. Serve over cooked fettuccine, if desired.

Makes 4 servings

Steak al Forno

Milanese Pork Chops

2 tablespoons all-purpose flour
½ teaspoon salt
½ teaspoon black pepper
1 egg
1 teaspoon water
¼ cup Italian seasoned dry bread crumbs
¼ cup grated Parmesan cheese
4 boneless pork loin chops, cut ¾ inch thick
1 tablespoon olive oil
1 tablespoon butter
   Lemon wedges

1. Preheat oven to 400°F. Combine flour, salt and pepper in shallow dish. Beat egg and water in shallow bowl. Combine bread crumbs and Parmesan in shallow plate.

2. Dip each pork chop to coat both sides evenly, first in flour mixture, then in egg mixture, then in bread crumb mixture. Press coating onto pork. Place on waxed paper; refrigerate 15 minutes. (Chops may be breaded and refrigerated up to 1 hour before cooking.)

3. Heat oil and butter in large ovenproof skillet over medium-high heat until butter is melted and bubbly. Add chops; cook 4 minutes on one side until golden brown. Turn chops; transfer skillet to oven. Bake 6 to 8 minutes or until chops are done (160°F). Serve with lemon.

Makes 4 servings

Milanese Pork Chops

The publisher would like to thank the companies and organizations listed below for the use of their recipes and photographs in this publication.

Bays English Muffin Corporation

BelGioioso® Cheese Inc.

Cabot® Creamery Cooperative

California Olive Industry

Cucina Classica Italiana, Inc.

Delmarva Poultry Industry, Inc.

Del Monte Corporation

Dole Food Company, Inc.

Filippo Berio® Olive Oil

Holland House®

McIlhenny Company (TABASCO® brand Pepper Sauce)

Perdue Farms Incorporated

Reckitt Benckiser Inc.

Riviana Foods Inc.

Unilever

Wisconsin Milk Marketing Board

metric conversion chart

VOLUME MEASUREMENTS (dry)

$^1/_8$ teaspoon = 0.5 mL
$^1/_4$ teaspoon = 1 mL
$^1/_2$ teaspoon = 2 mL
$^3/_4$ teaspoon = 4 mL
1 teaspoon = 5 mL
1 tablespoon = 15 mL
2 tablespoons = 30 mL
$^1/_4$ cup = 60 mL
$^1/_3$ cup = 75 mL
$^1/_2$ cup = 125 mL
$^2/_3$ cup = 150 mL
$^3/_4$ cup = 175 mL
1 cup = 250 mL
2 cups = 1 pint = 500 mL
3 cups = 750 mL
4 cups = 1 quart = 1 L

VOLUME MEASUREMENTS (fluid)

1 fluid ounce (2 tablespoons) = 30 mL
4 fluid ounces ($^1/_2$ cup) = 125 mL
8 fluid ounces (1 cup) = 250 mL
12 fluid ounces (1$^1/_2$ cups) = 375 mL
16 fluid ounces (2 cups) = 500 mL

WEIGHTS (mass)

$^1/_2$ ounce = 15 g
1 ounce = 30 g
3 ounces = 90 g
4 ounces = 120 g
8 ounces = 225 g
10 ounces = 285 g
12 ounces = 360 g
16 ounces = 1 pound = 450 g

DIMENSIONS

$^1/_{16}$ inch = 2 mm
$^1/_8$ inch = 3 mm
$^1/_4$ inch = 6 mm
$^1/_2$ inch = 1.5 cm
$^3/_4$ inch = 2 cm
1 inch = 2.5 cm

OVEN TEMPERATURES

250°F = 120°C
275°F = 140°C
300°F = 150°C
325°F = 160°C
350°F = 180°C
375°F = 190°C
400°F = 200°C
425°F = 220°C
450°F = 230°C

BAKING PAN SIZES

Utensil	Size in Inches/Quarts	Metric Volume	Size in Centimeters
Baking or Cake Pan (square or rectangular)	8×8×2	2 L	20×20×5
	9×9×2	2.5 L	23×23×5
	12×8×2	3 L	30×20×5
	13×9×2	3.5 L	33×23×5
Loaf Pan	8×4×3	1.5 L	20×10×7
	9×5×3	2 L	23×13×7
Round Layer Cake Pan	8×1½	1.2 L	20×4
	9×1½	1.5 L	23×4
Pie Plate	8×1¼	750 mL	20×3
	9×1¼	1 L	23×3
Baking Dish or Casserole	1 quart	1 L	—
	1½ quart	1.5 L	—
	2 quart	2 L	—